PATRON SAINT
OF
FIRST COMMUNICANTS

PATRON SAINT
OF
FIRST COMMUNICANTS

THE STORY OF
BLESSED IMELDA LAMBERTINI

By
Mary Fabyan Windeatt

Illustrated by
Gedge Harmon

TAN BOOKS AND PUBLISHERS, INC.
Rockford, Illinois 61105

IMPRIMI POTEST: ✠ Ignatius Esser, O.S.B.
                    Archabbot of St. Meinrad Archabbey

NIHIL OBSTAT: Gabriel Verkamp, O.S.B., S.T.D., Ph.D.
                    Censor Deputatus

IMPRIMATUR: ✠ Joseph E. Ritter, D.D.
                    Archbishop of St. Louis

First published in 1944, as "A Grail Publication," at St. Meinrad, Indiana, under the title *Little Sister: The Story of Blessed Imelda Lambertini, Patroness of First Communicants.*

ISBN-13: 978-0-89555-416-1
ISBN-10: 0-89555-416-X

Library of Congress Catalog Card No.: 90-71824

Printed and bound in the United States of America.

TAN BOOKS AND PUBLISHERS, INC.
P.O.Box 424
Rockford, Illinois 61105
1991

For
Rev. William LaVerdiere, S.S.S.

CONTENTS

PATRON SAINT
OF
FIRST COMMUNICANTS

CHAPTER ONE

A Child Is Born

HE blind basket-maker knew someone had stopped outside his door. His ears were very sharp and not a sound that echoed through the busy streets ever escaped him. Sometimes people felt that he really saw, so keen was his hearing, so dependable his memory. Then there were his baskets, shelves of them, deftly woven of colored reeds. It was hard to believe that they came from the hands of a man who could not see.

"It's the baker," he called out cheerfully. "Why don't you come inside, John?"

There was a deep laugh and the baker entered, a great hulk of a man, squeezing his way through the narrow entrance with difficulty.

1

"Some day I'll come so quietly that you'll never guess I'm here, Peter. But not today. Today I couldn't be quiet if I tried."

The blind man looked up curiously, while his thin fingers stopped their accustomed task of weaving reeds. "You sound as though you had good news, old friend. What is it?"

The baker put two loaves of bread on a nearby table, then clapped the blind man on the back. "My boy came home last night, Peter! What do you think of that?"

"*Philip came home?*"

"That's right. You know how we've all thought him dead these past five years. Well, he's not dead, Peter. He's very much alive. And he's made a tidy little fortune as a merchant in Algiers. Ah, if you only knew what it means to have him back again!"

The blind man smiled. He understood how his old friend had suffered. Young Philip, a boy of daring and rash spirits, had run away from home five years ago. No word had ever been heard of him since, and those in the city of Bologna who knew the baker were convinced the lad had come to no good.

"I'm very glad for you," said Peter simply. "I have no family but I can understand how you love Philip. And I'm quite sure. . . ."

"Yes?"

"That Philip is back only because of prayer."

A blank look struck the baker's face and he made a devout Sign of the Cross. "May God forgive me that I forgot to thank Him!" he murmured. "Of course, Peter. What else but prayer brought Philip back? Yours and mine. And perhaps there were others who thought of me in my trouble."

The blind man nodded. "Many others. It isn't for nothing that you give away bread to the poor, old friend. Be sure of that."

The baker shifted restlessly, his eyes upon a crucifix over the basket-maker's head. "I . . . I think I'll go to church a minute," he said lamely. "It seems only right that before the Blessed Sacrament I should make some kind of thanksgiving."

Peter laughed at the sudden concern in his friend's voice. "Are you afraid God will take your boy away again because you forgot to thank Him? Ah, John, yours is a common failing. We pray when we want something. We pray very hard indeed. But when our wish is granted, what do we do? Very little usually. And no one knows this better than I, who have so often failed my Maker. But come along. If you're going to church, I'll go with you. It's almost noon and I generally pay a visit at this time."

So the two men set out together down the narrow street—the one tall and strong, full of high spirits, the other stooped and grey, but with a face strongly marked with the peace of Christ. Their destination was the Dominican church a few blocks away, where the holy founder of the Dominican Order had been buried for over a hundred years.

"I can't stay very long," the baker whispered as they mounted the stone steps and approached the open door. "There's no one to watch my shop. But I want you to come tonight for supper, Peter. We're arranging a little celebration for Philip. You will be there, won't you?"

Peter smiled. "I'll be there. It's been many a day since I saw your boy."

Time passed. Far up the aisle, near the main altar, Peter arose from his knees and put away his rosary. He sensed that he was now alone in the church, and for a moment he considered whether he should not stay a little longer. Was it courteous to leave the King of Heaven without a single adorer? But presently a rustle of silk told him that some pious woman was about to take his place. Even now she was walking slowly up the aisle.

Peter gripped his cane in firm fingers and made his way to the door. The warm noon sunlight struck his face as he stepped outside, and he smiled at the pleasant feeling of warmth. June! It was a beautiful month. Always it was kind to the poor who must lodge in miserable quarters. It did not seek them out with the cruel fingers of frost.

With only slight hesitation, the blind man came down the church steps into the sunny street. As he turned resolutely to the right, away from his own shop, his mind was busy with a beautiful thought. It concerned the mercy of God the Father, Who allows sorrow to strike His children only for their own good. Sorrow, reflected Peter, is a powerful means to make souls remember that earth is not their true home. Sorrow, bravely borne, is nothing more than a key to the wonders of heaven.

"In heaven, my good friend John will be happier than he is at his son's return," thought Peter. "Even I, a blind man, will be able to see beautiful things."

Slowly the basket-maker walked through the June sunshine, his cane beating out a gentle rhythm on the cobblestones. Sometimes a familiar voice greeted him, and he stopped for a brief chat with an old friend. But he heeded no invitation to rest himself, to stop for food and drink. He was interested in only one thing. He wanted to reach the palace of the Captain General of Bologna. Egano Lambertini might be a wealthy man, powerful in government circles, but he was not proud. He always had time for the poor. And it was the same with his wife, Donna Castora. The two were Christians in the real sense.

"Perhaps I'm wrong," thought Peter, as he tapped his way slowly along the street, "but I have a feeling that Donna Castora has much to do with Philip's return. It was only a few months ago that she came to my shop and bought a few baskets. I told her then of John's sorrow and she promised to pray for his boy. Now it seems only right that someone should go to her and say that her prayer is answered."

As the blind man turned into the spacious avenue leading toward the Lambertini castle, the air was suddenly filled with the pealing of bells. It was a joyous sound, and Peter looked up curiously. The bells were not church bells. They were those of the castle. He could almost see them swinging in the grey stone towers.

"What's happened?" cried an excited voice from a shop door.

The question was immediately taken up by others —merchants, children, beggars, wives who had been busy in their kitchens. Of a sudden the street was a beehive of excitement as people rushed out to gaze at the grey castle on the hill where flocks of startled pigeons were circling through the air.

"It's good news of some sort!" someone cried. "Maybe Donna Castora has had a son!"

"A son for the Captain General!" put in another voice. "God be praised!"

THEY SURGED UP THE BROAD AVENUE.

As though a signal had been given, a flood of men and women began to surge up the broad avenue. Prominent in the motley procession were beggars, dozens of them, roused from their usual corners by the clamor of the bells. If it were true that Egano Lambertini now had a son, he would be more generous than ever with his alms. Perhaps a jug of wine to each man who wished the child well? Or a loaf of fine white bread?

"Out of the way, blind man!" someone shouted. "I want to reach the castle first."

To escape being trampled, Peter hastily moved into the recess of a deserted doorway. To some the blind basket-maker might present a pitiable sight, shabby and frail and forgotten, but Peter was far from feeling sad. Egano Lambertini, the Captain General of Bologna, Ambassador to the Republic of Venice, had been given a son and heir!

"He deserves good fortune," the blind man thought. "He and his wife have always been kind to everyone."

For half an hour Peter stood in the doorway, waiting for his sharp ears to tell him that the crowd had thinned and that now he might make his own way safely to the castle. When the moment finally arrived, he moved slowly into the street. The bells were still pealing joyfully and his heart sang with them. He had started this trip in order to speak briefly to Donna Castora, to thank her for her prayers on behalf of the baker's missing boy. Such news, he felt, would make the good woman happy. But now his little errand was hardly necessary. Donna Castora was having her own moment of triumph. The news of Philip's return must be told at some other time.

"I'll go to the castle anyway," thought Peter. "Not that I am needed. No one would miss me if I stayed away. But it will be good to have some little part in the merrymaking."

The basket-maker had just turned into the road that ran by the back of the castle when he heard a group of people approaching. They were in high spirits and apparently carried away with them a goodly supply of food and drink from the celebration.

"I say it's a shame!" cried one man, taking no notice of Peter. "Who started the story that the Captain General had a son?"

"Who cares?" sang out a companion. "I say a girl is as good as a boy when she brings us presents like these!"

"You lie, friend! Daughters only cause a man trouble. Believe me, I ought to know. Haven't I six of them?"

Puzzled, the blind man stepped back to let the

noisy group pass. So it was a baby girl who had come to grace the Lambertini household instead of a boy! Then why were the bells pealing so loud and long? This was a custom usually reserved for the first-born son of a noble family.

"I'll go and see," Peter told himself. But as he hurried along the road, his trusty cane finding the smoothest part, he could not agree with the speaker who had just passed. Whether boy or girl, Donna Castora's child possessed a soul that the saving waters of Baptism soon would render spotless and beautiful. This soul could never die. It would live forever.

"Father in heaven, bless this little newcomer!" said Peter fervently. "Help her to be Your faithful servant."

Soon he had reached the rear courtyard, filled now to overflowing with the poor of Bologna. Here long tables had been hastily set up, and servants were busy bringing forth food and drink. At one side a few musicians, in festive attire of red and gold, tuned their strings.

"This way, friend," said a servant woman's kindly voice. "Hurry, or you'll not find a place."

Peter nodded and let himself be taken by the arm. As he sat down at one of the tables, a great shout of applause went up from the happy crowd.

"Long live the Captain General!" cried the assembly. "Long live his wife and child!"

The basket-maker turned his sightless eyes toward the front of the courtyard. It was evident that Egano Lambertini had arrived to greet his guests and bid them have their fill. Probably he would soon announce the day of Baptism, when another celebration would be in order for Bologna's poor. Happily Peter settled himself to listen, to learn by what name the little one would be called, to pledge his prayers for her health and happiness.

CHAPTER TWO

THE DREAM

HE Captain General lost no time in declaring that his daughter's Baptism would take place the following Sunday. His wife's brother, Egidio Galuzzi, Archbishop of Crete, was expected in Bologna in a day or two, and he would perform the ceremony.

"The child will be called Imelda," announced the Captain General happily, "and you will be most welcome at the castle on that day. Now, friends and fellow-citizens, make merry as you will!"

There was another burst of applause for the Captain General's words, and then the crowd settled down to the unaccustomed treat of free food and wine. The celebration continued for several hours, even after darkness had set in, for colored flares lit up the castle grounds and there seemed to be no end to the poor and crippled who streamed through the gates.

Listening to the sounds of revelry far below her window, Donna Castora smiled.

"The whole city is celebrating because God has sent me a little girl," she thought. "How glad I am, too!"

Presently the mother closed her eyes and in a few minutes was deep in slumber. But she did not realize that she slept. It seemed that she was abroad in the familiar streets of Bologna. It was morning, a mild and sunny morning in mid-May. Plainly visible in the bright sunshine were the Cathedral of Saint Peter and the various towers and monuments erected to the city's nobility. But how strange! She glimpsed no familiar face, and even the dress of those about her was of a peculiar fashion. It seemed to belong to another century than her own.

Presently a number of young men passed by, clad in the drab grey of the Franciscan Order. Here, at least, was a familiar sight. Donna Castora eagerly scanned the faces of the young friars, giving alms to those nearest, for it was evident they were on a begging tour for the poor. Alas! There was no one she recognized. Nor did she see a face she knew among the beggars, the children, the students laughing and chattering on their way to and from the University. She was truly a stranger in Bologna—the city of her birth!

Suddenly there was a commotion in the distance. The people in the street stopped to look up curiously. "What is it?" one asked the other. "Who is coming?"

Donna Castora also stopped, staring off at the great square before the Cathedral. Then she saw a strange sight. Many friars, clad in black and white habits, were approaching the Dominican convent. At their head walked a slightly-built man with reddish-brown hair. His eyes lingered lovingly on the people in the street, and somehow it seemed as though a light shone from his forehead. It was like a star, and Donna Castora suddenly found herself upon her knees. Those nearby also knelt, whereupon the leader of the black-and-white-clad figures raised his hand in fatherly blessing. Then, still smiling, still with the strange radiance playing about his head, he passed through the doorway of the Dominican convent.

"It's Father Dominic de Guzman, the founder of the Friars Preachers!" thought Donna Castora, although how she knew this she could not tell. Nor could she explain how she also knew that the celebrated preacher had come to Bologna from Viterbo to hold the first general meeting of his friars. All she knew was that her eyes had rested upon a saint.

FATHER DOMINIC GAVE HIS BLESSING.

Slowly the dream faded. The streets of Bologna, so familiar and yet so strange, vanished. Once more Donna Castora found herself gazing at the walls of her own room. The courtyard below still rang with the sound of merrymaking, but the woman scarcely heard it. Her heart was pounding wildly. What was the meaning of this strange dream? Why had she found herself transported to a spring day in the year 1220 when Dominic de Guzman was in Bologna to hold the first General Chapter of his newly-formed Order?

"He looked at me so kindly," she thought. "It was almost as though he gave me a more special blessing than the others."

Slowly she reached out a hand and rang a little bell on the table beside her. Immediately a serving woman appeared.

"Yes, my lady? You wanted something?"

"Yes, Beatrice. Will you bring the baby here? I want to look at her again."

The serving woman bowed and disappeared, returning presently with the newborn child wrapped in the softest of white wool. "She is asleep now, my lady, the little dear! But when her eyes are open, they are as blue as the ocean. Ah, but she's a beauty! Somehow I feel great things are in store for this little one."

The mother held out her arms. "Imelda!" she mur-

mured lovingly. "Are great things in store for you?"
Time passed, and Beatrice looked anxiously at
her mistress. "Perhaps I'd better take the child now,"
she suggested. "You're tired, my lady, and should
have some rest."
Donna Castora gave up the baby reluctantly. "All
right," she said. "I believe I could sleep now."
For a moment the serving woman cradled the
child in her arms, then cast a doubtful glance at the
open window. The crowd in the courtyard below was
singing lustily now, the gay folk tunes that everyone
knew. More than that. They were beating out the
rhythm with their hands and feet.
"You can't sleep with all that noise, my lady. Shall
I send word to the kitchen that it's time for the people to go home?"
Donna Castora laughed. "No, no, Beatrice! After
all, haven't they promised to pray for Imelda? And
for her father and mother? Let the poor folk have
their fun."
The serving woman nodded doubtfully. "Very well,
my lady. Good night to you now. I'll see that no harm
comes to this precious little one."
When the door had shut behind her trusted friend
and servant, Donna Castora sighed happily. She
was tired. It would be good to go to sleep. Perhaps
she would even dream again of Father Dominic de

Guzman. But though she tried to relax, to recapture the smile and blessing of the saint, it was impossible. A hundred thoughts chased one another around her brain. Imelda! Imelda! What would the future bring this newborn child? Was Beatrice right? Were her own suspicions right? Did God have some great work for such a little girl to do?

"Perhaps she will be a nun," thought Donna Castora. "Maybe some day she will go to Saint Agnes' convent here in Bologna and ask for the Dominican habit. What a heavenly place that is! And how many saints have lived there!"

She was pondering these thoughts, and smiling at them, too, when a great roar went up from the courtyard below. The gay folk songs had suddenly given place to shouts of welcome, to cheers. Apparently some important person was arriving at the castle gate.

Donna Castora became tense. "He's come!" she thought. "God be praised! Egidio has come far earlier than we expected!"

Quickly her hand found the bell on the table and rang it vigorously. "Beatrice!" she called. "Beatrice! Come here!"

At once the door opened and the serving woman appeared, a flickering candle held high above her head. Her face was anxious.

"What is it, my lady? What's wrong?"

"IMELDA," SHE MURMURED LOVINGLY.

Donna Castora's eyes were bright with excitement. "Nothing's wrong, Beatrice. But the Archbishop has come, hasn't he? He's downstairs now?" The serving woman was reproachful. "His Grace has arrived, my lady. That's true. But you should be asleep. You promised me an hour ago that you would take some rest."

"I know. But I want to see the Archbishop, Beatrice. After all, he's my brother. And I have so many things to ask him about Imelda. You see, I had a dream a while ago, a most wonderful dream. It was about Saint Dominic. I saw him walking along the street. He blessed all of us who stood watching him, but to me he seemed to give a very special blessing. I think maybe it was because . . . oh, Beatrice! Please go and bring my brother here!"

The serving woman sighed. "Very well, my lady. I'll give His Grace your message."

Egidio Galuzzi, Archbishop of Crete, was weary after his long sea voyage to Venice. The overland trip to Padua, Ferrara and Bologna had not been easy, either. Yet he was as anxious as his sister for a few brief words and willingly accompanied Beatrice to the bedchamber. Here, seated in an elaborately carved chair, his feet resting upon a pillow of red velvet, he listened patiently to the story of the dream.

"It does mean something, doesn't it?" Donna

Castora asked eagerly. "Ah, Egidio, you know all about theology. Don't you think God sometimes sends a dream for some special purpose?"

The Archbishop smiled. "It has happened," he said. "The Wise Men were warned in a dream to return to their own countries without visiting Herod a second time. The good Saint Joseph also had a dream wherein he learned that his spouse would be the Mother of God. Yes, Castora, sometimes dreams are Heaven-sent."

"And this one of mine? Egidio, don't you think it came for a special reason? Don't you think the good Saint Dominic blessed me as he did because of . . . of Imelda? Surely he meant that some day she would be great among his followers?"

"We must not be rash about these things," said the Archbishop carefully. "Every child born into the world is given the grace to become a saint. Castora, you must teach little Imelda this truth and help her to use the graces God gives her. When you have done this task well, there will be time enough to decide about your dream."

The eyes of the woman rested pleadingly upon her brother as he rose to his feet. "Don't go just yet," she begged softly. "I know you must be tired, Egidio, but if you talk to me a little while I may be able to fall asleep. That would please Beatrice."

There was an amused smile on the face of the Archbishop. "But what shall I talk about? Myself? My trip? Dear sister, such things would be better saved for tomorrow. And remember—I haven't seen my little niece yet."

"I know. But talk to me now about Saint Dominic. Then you can see the baby."

The Archbishop settled himself once more in the carved wooden chair. "This is the year 1322," he began. "Saint Dominic has been dead since 1221. He is buried here in Bologna. His friars are known throughout all Europe as preachers and teachers, and I am happy to be numbered among them."

"Go on," whispered the woman sleepily. "Tell me about his nuns."

"Saint Dominic's first nuns were nine French noblewomen. They were converted from heresy by the good man's preaching in 1206. The Bishop of Prouille, in France, gave them a convent there, and from then on their great aim in life was to pray for the success of Dominic and his friars. In 1219 Dominic founded a second convent in Madrid, and a few months later he arrived in Rome to attract more women to the religious life."

Presently the Archbishop paused and glanced at his sister. Heaven be praised! Castora had fallen asleep at last!

CHAPTER THREE

ANOTHER BIRTHDAY

S TIME passed, little Imelda gave signs that God had blessed her with many gifts. For one thing, she was an extremely pretty child. For another, she had a quick mind. Lastly, she was truly unselfish. From the time she was able to walk and talk, she showed a great interest in making other people happy. It was indeed a glorious day when she was allowed to come to the kitchen and assist in giving out food and clothing to the poor.

One June morning, as the Captain General's small daughter sat playing in a sunny corner of the garden, a wonderful thought came into her mind. It was her fifth birthday, and many colored flags were flying from the castle towers in honor of the great event.

"I know why it's nice to help other people," she told herself happily. "It's because God is living in them! When we help the poor and sick, we're really helping Him!"

A brown thrush perched atop a rose bush turned a bright eye on the little girl, then burst into lilting song.

"You're right!" he trilled. "You're very right!"

Imelda was delighted. What a wonderful thing it was to be alive! Even little children could give honor and glory to God. They could remember that every human body is meant to be the dwelling of the Most Blessed Trinity. Because of this, they could be kind and obedient to those around them. And for the millions of people they would never see or know, other temples of God, they could offer little prayers and sacrifices.

Presently Imelda knelt down, folded her hands and closed her eyes devoutly. In a dress of the finest white silk, with her golden curls tumbling about her shoulders, she seemed like some small and very beautiful statue. The pretty sight was quite lost upon Beatrice, however, when she came down to the garden a few minutes later. Indeed, the serving woman uttered a little cry of dismay.

"Miss Imelda! What are you doing? Why are you kneeling on the damp ground?"

Slowly the small statue came to life and the child looked up. "I was just thinking of something nice, Beatrice."

"And what's that?"

"I was thinking that I'm a Tabernacle."

"A *what?*"

"A Tabernacle. Yes, because God has been inside me ever since I was baptized. You're a Tabernacle, too, Beatrice. And Father and Mother . . . and my uncle . . . and all the good people in the whole world. Isn't it wonderful?"

The serving woman smiled broadly. "I suppose it is, child. But you don't have to kneel on the damp ground to be a Tabernacle. Come, now—it's time you went back to the house. There's going to be a really fine dinner in honor of your birthday, you know."

Imelda nodded. "I'll come with you, Beatrice. But just think! I've been a Tabernacle for five years. And I never really understood about it until now."

The serving woman smiled again. "Bless you!" she murmured. "What big thoughts you have in that little head!"

After dinner, which was an elaborate affair served on golden dishes, Imelda went with her parents to a small room on the top floor of the castle. The walls were hung with rich tapestries brought from Turkey and Persia. The tables and chairs were hand-carved of rare wood, many inlaid with ivory, pearl and jade. Freshly-cut flowers were everywhere, and though it was June a huge fire was burning on the hearth to drive away any possible chill from the stone walls and floor.

"We have some surprises for you," said Egano Lambertini, surveying his little daughter with affection. "Come here, child. Open the packages from your friends."

Imelda ran eagerly to a large table, heaped high with gifts. "Oh, Father! How many there are!"

"Of course. Many people love my little girl."

Donna Castora came forward to help the child undo the packages. "Even the King of Naples sent you something," she said happily. "Imelda dear, you must remember to pray very hard for such good friends."

The child shook her curls. "I'll pray every day," she said.

For several minutes the parents stood by as their five-year-old daughter delightedly discovered one after another of her gifts. There were toys, pictures, jewelry, silks, perfumes—the whole worth a small fortune. Finally, when each package had been opened, Imelda held up a rosary made of large white pearls. From it hung a golden crucifix.

"Oh, Mother! How lovely this is!"

Donna Castora flushed with pleasure. "That's my

little gift to you," she whispered. "It was given to me by my own mother when I was your age."

Imelda caressed the beads gently. How beautiful they were—and how the golden crucifix sparkled in the light of the fire!

"I love the Rosary," she said. "I'll offer it every day to Our Lady."

The Captain General rattled his sword and cleared his throat. "And what about my present?" he asked. "Little daughter, don't you see those yards of fine silk? They will make you seem even prettier than you are."

Imelda turned to look at the silks—pale blue, rose, green, yellow, white—all the way from the Orient. So rare and precious! Later on they would be made into dresses for her.

"They're lovely!" she exclaimed. "Oh, Father—you're so good to me!"

Egano Lambertini chuckled. "And why not? You're a good child. You deserve the best."

For a moment Imelda was silent, looking at the gifts piled high on the table. Then her eyes dropped to the gleaming string of pearls in her hand.

"What's the trouble?" asked Donna Castora, as the child's face grew wistful. "Is something wrong?"

Imelda quickly shook her head. "Oh, no. I was just wondering . . . now that I'm five years old. . . ."

"COULD I HAVE JUST ONE MORE PRESENT?"

"Yes? What is it, child?"

"I was wondering if I could have just one more present, Mother. It wouldn't cost anything . . . and it would be so nice . . . better than any of these lovely things. . . ."

The Captain General laughed. "Greedy girl! What more do you want than this?"

Imelda lifted her blue eyes. Her small face was suddenly very solemn. "I'd like to receive Our Lord in Holy Communion," she whispered. "Just like grown-up people do."

There was a moment of astonished silence. Then Donna Castora dropped to her knees and enfolded her little one in an affectionate embrace. "I'm afraid that can't be, dear."

"But why not, Mother? If Our Lord loved little children when He was on earth, surely He still wants them to come to Him?"

"Of course He does. But you see there are rules about receiving Holy Communion. For one thing, a person must be old enough to understand the great honor."

"I'm five years old today. And I do understand. Truly!"

Egano Lambertini shifted awkwardly. He had always felt that his little daughter was no ordinary child. Now the sight of her small figure, tense with holy desire, was too much for him.

"You'll have to be fourteen years old before you can receive Holy Communion," he declared flatly. "That's a rule of the Church, so don't bother your mother any more. Just be grateful for all these nice presents."

Imelda twined the pearl rosary about her arm and moved obediently toward the table. There were tears in her eyes, for never had she heard her father speak so abruptly.

"I didn't mean to be greedy," she said in a quivering voice. "It's only that I don't want to wait any longer for Our Lord to come into my heart."

The Captain General softened. "The time will soon pass," he muttered gruffly. "You'll be fourteen years old before you know it, and the prettiest girl in Bologna. Now cheer up, child. This is a day for happiness, not tears."

There was a sudden knock at the door, and Beatrice entered. In her hand she carried a small green basket covered with a white cloth.

"Peter the blind man sent this for Miss Imelda's birthday," she informed Donna Castora. "John the baker made the little cakes. Both men give you their greetings, my lady."

The interruption was well-timed, and Donna Castora threw a quick glance at her husband over Imelda's head.

"Are the men still here, Beatrice?"

"Yes, my lady. They are having something to eat and drink in the kitchen."

Donna Castora looked at her small daughter. "How would you like to say 'thank you' to John and Peter for their gifts?" she asked.

"All right, Mother," said Imelda slowly. "Maybe the blind man would tell me a story, too. He seems to know so many."

Donna Castora smiled in relief. "Then run along with Beatrice, child. Your father and I have some things to talk about."

With her hand in that of the trusted serving woman, Imelda went quickly through the stone corridors of the castle, down many winding stairways, and finally entered the great kitchen. Here enormous black iron kettles were simmering over the open fire. The air was filled with a hundred spicy scents, and on a nearby table were stacked golden mounds of freshly baked bread. As usual, the Lambertini kitchen was ready for whatever crowd of poor should come to the castle gate.

Imelda lost no time in spotting her two friends. The baker and the basket-maker were seated near the door, engaged in conversation over their bread and cheese. Both rose to greet the child as Beatrice led her forward.

"A happy birthday, little one!" cried the blind man, reaching out his hand. "May you have many more!" "And may they all find you in good health," the baker added shyly.

Imelda sat down on the small stool which Beatrice had brought and looked at her two friends. "The little basket is very pretty, Peter. And the cakes look good, too, John. It was so nice of you both to remember me."

The basket-maker turned his sightless eyes on the child. "You must have received many gifts that are much finer than ours," he said gently. "What is the best one, little friend?"

Imelda looked at the strand of white pearls still twined about her arm. "A rosary," she said slowly. "It's made of pearls and has a golden crucifix. My Mother gave it to me." Then, with an understanding glance at the baker, she turned again to the blind man.

"Would you tell me a little story, Peter? A special one for my birthday?"

The blind man laughed. "Another story, child? I think you must know all my poor tales by now."

"Oh, no, Peter! Beatrice says there's no better storyteller in all Bologna than you. You know dozens of them."

"He knows hundreds," corrected the baker boastfully. "When my own boy was a little lad he was always bothering Peter for stories."

The blind man laughed again. "I could tell you the story of Tarcisius," he said. "Maybe you would like that one."

Imelda's blue eyes opened wide. "*Tarcisius*, Peter? Who is he?"

The blind man folded his lean fingers. "He is a Saint, little friend. A brave Roman boy who was not afraid to die for the love of God. Do you think you'd like to hear about him?"

Imelda nodded. "Oh, yes!" she cried eagerly. "I'm sure I would!"

CHAPTER FOUR

THE DOMINICANS IN BOLOGNA

HE story of Tarcisius, who had lost his life during the Christian persecutions, ever remained a favorite with Imelda. Often she would close her eyes and try to imagine what this Roman boy had been like.

"I'm sure he had many friends," she told herself. "And I'm sure he was wonderfully happy when the priest allowed him to carry the Blessed Sacrament to those who were afraid to come to Mass. Oh, why couldn't I have been alive during the persecutions? Maybe the priest would have let me carry Our Lord, too. They needed many helpers, those brave Christians whom the Emperor hated so much!"

Imelda had another heavenly friend besides

Tarcisius. This was the martyr Agnes, who had given her life for the Faith at the age of twelve. Yes, these two children of the Catacombs were real friends of the Captain General's small daughter. They were her imaginary companions, and often she asked them to help her to love God as He wished to be loved. What did it matter that hundreds of years separated the three of them? That Tarcisius and Agnes slept in martyrs' graves while Imelda Lambertini was very much alive? The doctrine of the Communion of Saints set aside time and place. In God's plan, the souls in heaven and in purgatory are united in a wonderful brotherhood with the faithful on earth. There is a constant flow of understanding and encouragement, binding all three.

"I must remember this," Imelda told herself frequently. "Dear Tarcisius, dear Agnes, please let other people have this same thought. It may help them when troubles come."

So the years passed, and Egano Lambertini's only daughter had her seventh birthday, her eighth, her ninth. Yet she still was not allowed to receive Holy Communion. The custom of the time did not permit children so young—even when they knew the Catechism perfectly—to approach the Holy Table. And try though he would, the Archbishop of Crete could do nothing to help his little niece in her great

disappointment. The only bit of advice he could give
she already knew by heart.

*"Wait until you are fourteen, Imelda. Our Lord
will come then. I promise it."*

Five more years! It seemed such a long time to
Imelda! So many things could happen before her
fourteenth birthday! For instance, she might have
some serious accident and die! But she remained
silent, in spite of such doubts, and asked for the
great favor no more. After all, it must be God's Will
that she remain away from Him these five years.
The thing to do was to bear the disappointment
bravely and trust that He would let everything turn
to good.

"He has a reason for making me wait," she
thought. "Some day I'll understand what it is."

The Lambertini family was well-known throughout Bologna for its kindness to poor religious.
Among the monasteries and convents which experi-
enced this charity was that of Saint Agnes—a house
of cloistered Dominican nuns. The tale of how
Dominican life had first started here, as well as in
the friars' convent in Bologna, never failed to hold
Imelda's attention. Like her mother, she had an
intense admiration for the Order of Preachers, and
this was fostered in many ways by her saintly uncle,
the Archbishop of Crete.

One morning Beatrice was called upon to act as audience while Imelda related the familiar story once more.

"Saint Dominic sent his first friars here in 1218," the little girl explained. "Do you know why, Beatrice?"

The serving woman, well knowing how to play her part, shook her head innocently. "Why, child?"

"Because Bologna had such a famous University. Students came here from all over Europe, just as they do now, to study law. There were many clever professors at the University, and Saint Dominic knew that if his friars could make these men good Christians, the students would follow the same course. So he ordered one of his dear friends, a French friar named Father Reginald, to come and help start a convent near the University."

"I've heard about him," put in Beatrice, warming to the little game. "They called him Master Reginald of Orleans. He was a wonderful preacher."

"Yes, Beatrice. Father Reginald was a wonderful preacher. Crowds came to hear him whenever he spoke at the Cathedral, or in the Square. And because he was so clever and so good, he did a grand work for God. He converted hundreds of students and teachers at the University. And he brought many vocations to the Dominican friars, too."

As she was telling the story of the brilliant Father

Reginald, Imelda, as usual, lost all track of time. It seemed as though she were truly transported across the years to those pioneer days in Bologna when Dominican life was something new for everyone. But Father Reginald, important though he was, figured in only part of the story. Having described his enormous success in bringing vocations to the Dominican Order, Imelda drew in another heroic soul.

"These first Dominican friars were living in a house attached to the little church of Saint Mary," she declared. "Beatrice, the place was far too small for so many priests and Brothers. Finally they looked about for another house and church and decided that one called 'Saint Nicholas in the Vineyards' would suit them. It was outside the city walls in a beautifully quiet place. So what did they do?"

The serving woman responded smilingly. "They asked the d'Andalo family, who owned the property, to let them have it, child. But this family wouldn't agree. They were rather angry with the Dominicans because of the friars' influence over one of their daughters."

"Yes, Beatrice," Imelda replied approvingly. "That's the way it was. Diana d'Andalo had been so carried away by Father Reginald's sermons that she wanted to be a nun. She was very beautiful and very wealthy, but these things didn't count for much with Diana.

She wanted to be a Dominican, too, and help Father Reginald and the other friars by a life of prayer. Finally she managed to calm her family's feelings and they allowed the friars to take possession of 'Saint Nicholas in the Vineyards.' "

To complete the story of how Dominican life had come to Bologna always took Imelda considerable time. First, there was the matter of Father Reginald and his marvelous success as a preacher. Then there was the case of Diana d'Andalo. Despite objections from her wealthy family, the latter had run away from home at the age of nineteen to the Augustinian convent of Ronzano. Here she hoped to remain while plans were being made for the foundation of a Dominican monastery for women. Alas! Diana's father and brothers were furious at the step she had taken. They stormed the convent of Ronzano and dragged her home by force. In the struggle, she suffered a broken rib and other injuries. After this her health declined. She was kept a prisoner at home, and no Dominican friar was allowed anywhere near the family castle.

"How she must have suffered!" sighed Imelda. "Oh, Beatrice! I always feel so sad when I think of this part of the story!"

"But it turned out well in the end, child. Don't forget that."

IMELDA BEGAN HER FAVORITE STORY.

"I know. But Diana had to wait two years before her family would let her be a nun. And in the meantime the two friars she loved most of all died. Imagine, Beatrice, what it would have meant to lose friends like Father Reginald and Saint Dominic. Don't you think Diana felt very lonely after their deaths, even though she could be glad they were in heaven?"

Beatrice shifted uneasily. She had always admired the remarkable memory of her nine-year-old charge, yet sometimes she grew a little worried at the child's great interest in Bologna's saints. This story of the Dominicans, for instance. It wasn't meant that a little girl should think too long or too often about it. It was far beyond her years.

"I suppose so, child. But let's not worry about such things now. Those good souls are saints in heaven today. And Diana is famous because she founded the first convent of Dominican nuns here. I'm sure she wouldn't want you to be unhappy over the sad part of her life."

Imelda agreed. "You're right, Beatrice. But tell me something."

"What, little one?"

"When are we going to visit the Sisters at Saint Agnes' again? It's been such a long time since we took them any food."

The serving woman was glad to change the subject. "I think we're going today, Miss Imelda. Do you want to come along?"

The child's eyes grew bright. "Oh, yes!" she cried eagerly. "You know I love to visit the Sisters, Beatrice. And maybe afterwards we could go to see the basket-maker. You said he wasn't so well these days."

A shadow crossed the woman's face. "That's right. Peter has rheumatism, and they say he hasn't worked at his weaving for weeks. Poor soul! How can he make a living if he doesn't work?"

Imelda hesitated. "Do you know that I pray for him every day?" she asked shyly. "And do you know what I ask God to do for my good old friend?"

"Cure him of his rheumatism, I hope. It's really serious."

The child shook her head. "I ask for more than that. Beatrice, I ask God to give Peter back his sight! Oh, I know it means a miracle, but what does that matter? God can do anything He chooses!"

Later in the day a luxurious carriage stopped before the plain stone building that was the convent of Saint Agnes and three figures alighted. The first of these was Donna Castora. Beatrice followed, carrying two heavy baskets covered with a white cloth. Then came Imelda, in a blue silk dress with a black lace veil caught over her golden curls. As the three stood upon the sidewalk, a thin sound of chanting reached their ears. Hearing it, the child looked up anxiously.

"Mother, we won't be able to talk to the Sisters!"

Donna Castora smiled. "Not for a little while, Imelda. They're saying Vespers just now. But we can go in the church and wait until they have finished. As for the baskets, Beatrice, perhaps you'd better take them to the lay Sister at the door? She won't be at prayers like the others."

"Yes, my lady," said the serving woman. "And I have an idea the good soul will be very happy about your generous gift. After all, the poor Sisters, Heaven bless them, don't have many friends like you."

Presently Imelda was kneeling beside her mother in the small public chapel attached to the convent. How peaceful it was here! There was no sound save the sweet voices of the nuns as they chanted the Psalms of the Divine Office. Imelda knelt very still and straight, her eyes upon the Tabernacle. Her mind was busy with many thoughts. One of these concerned the nuns, hidden now by the double iron grating that closed their chapel from public view. What had led them to be shut away like this from the world? Why did they spend hour after hour in

THEY WERE GOING TO VISIT THE NUNS.

chanting the Divine Praises, in humble labors with
their hands, when they might have enjoyed a com-
fortable life in the world?

"It's because they love God so much," the little girl
decided. "They want to give Him the best of all gifts,
so they give themselves. They give their freedom.
They give their hearts. And now they pray for those
who are too selfish to make such gifts. Dear Lord,
there must be thousands of sinners saved from hell
because of the generosity of the Sisters!"

Soon the chanting ceased, and at a sign from
Donna Castora Imelda rose to her feet. Vespers was
over. Now they could spend a little while with the
Prioress in the convent parlor. But though the child
followed her mother toward the door, her eyes lingered on an altar at the side of the church. Many
candles were burning here, and the freshly-cut flowers with which it was decked filled the air with fragrance.

Imelda looked lovingly at the little shrine and at
the Latin inscription carved in the front of the altar.
How well she knew these words! Years ago her uncle
had explained what they meant. Now she quickly
spelled them out again.

Here lies Sister Diana d'Andalo
who made the vows of religion in the
hands of
Blessed Dominic
and built the Monastery of Saint Agnes
in which
she lived most holily for thirteen years
and migrated to the Lord in the year 1236.

"How I wish I could have known the blessed Diana!" thought Imelda wistfully. "And how I wish I could love Our Lord as these Sisters do! Maybe then He would come to me in Holy Communion!"

CHAPTER FIVE

A NEW LIFE

MELDA often visited other religious houses in and around Bologna. One of these was the convent of Saint Mary Magdalen, on a hill outside the city known as Val-di-Pietra. It was an ancient place, built several centuries before by the children of Saint Benedict. Later it had been given to the nuns of the Order of Saint Mark. Since 1299, however, cloistered Dominican nuns had lived here.

This convent was close to Imelda's thoughts. She had a great desire to save souls, and it seemed that the Holy Spirit was urging her to set about this task more fruitfully by giving herself to the religious life. What if she was only nine years old? In the fourteenth century even very small children entered monasteries and convents. Such places were schools of the Lord's service.

"Mother, I want to be a nun," the little girl declared one day. "I want to live at Val-di-Pietra with the Sisters."

Donna Castora received the announcement with mixed feelings. She had never forgotten the dream after Imelda's birth wherein she had been given Saint Dominic's blessing. As the memory came to her mind again and again, she had grown more certain that the holy man was claiming her child for his Order. In the beginning she had been thrilled and grateful, but now her mother's heart rebelled at being separated from her little one. After all, the child was so young! How could she endure the hardships of the cloister?

"Darling, wait a little while," she urged. "You know the Sisters are much older than you. And stronger. It wouldn't be right to go there and be a trouble to them."

Imelda listened respectfully, but her mind was made up. God wanted her at Val-di-Pietra. She was sure of that. Quickly she enlisted the aid of her uncle, the Dominican Archbishop; of her father's saintly sister, the Abbess Massima; of another uncle who was an Augustinian priest. To all these, as well as to her father, she described her ardent desire to be a religious and thus gain many souls for Heaven. Then she added gravely that there was another important reason for wishing to go to the convent. If she were a nun, surely she would be allowed to receive Holy Communion?

The Captain General and his wife had many long and sorrowful talks before they reached a decision. They loved Imelda dearly, but was it right to keep her at home when to all appearances God was calling her to His own service? Finally the Captain gave in.

"Other parents give their children, Castora. Are we to be less generous?"

The mother was tearful. Imelda was the child of so many prayers! For years after their marriage they had waited for God to send her to them. Now how could they give her to the difficult life of the cloister?

"Imelda's not used to hardships," insisted Donna Castora. "She's always been surrounded with luxury. Oh, Egano! What if she should *die* at Val-di-Pietra?"

The Captain General soothed his wife's anxious feelings as best he could. Yes, the life of a Dominican nun was hard. She was shut away from the world by an iron grating. Sometimes food was scarce. There were long hours of prayer and work. Never could she come outside for a little vacation with friends and family. Yet was not God full of kindness and mercy? If He wished their little one to serve Him in the cloister, He would give her the necessary strength.

In the end Donna Castora yielded, to Imelda's great delight, and a few weeks later came the wonderful day when the nuns agreed to receive her. As the nine-year-old girl looked upon her castle home for the last time, her heart filled with a grief which was very natural. Although it was good to be called to God's service, it was also difficult. She loved her parents so much, her friends among the poor! Then there was Beatrice, the kindly serving woman who had watched over her from babyhood. It was going to be hard to leave these dear ones forever.

"This is the first sacrifice in my new life," she thought. "Dear Lord, will You use it to help some poor sinner?"

On the day and at the hour agreed upon, the new candidate arrived at Val-di-Pietra. As she embraced her parents for the last time, the child made a real effort not to cry.

"I'll never be very far away from you, Mother," she whispered. "Please don't feel lonely."

Donna Castora did not guess the heartbreak in her little daughter's words. She could think of only one thing. *Far from feeling sad, she was actually happy that Imelda was going to be a religious!* The great gift had come to her the night before, when Saint Dominic had blessed her in another dream. Once again she had seen him smile, and in an instant her worried heart had known peace. The saint had made her understand that her little girl would do great things for souls.

"Good-bye, dear," she murmured. "I'm so proud of you!"

The Captain General was deeply moved. "I'm proud, too," he said. "May God bless you always, child!"

There was no time for long speeches. As the cloister door opened, Imelda took a deep breath and walked firmly across the threshold. Not once did she falter. As the door softly closed behind her, a white-clad figure came forward with outstretched arms.

"Welcome, child! A thousand welcomes!"

Imelda returned the embrace eagerly. It was the Mother Prioress with whom she had often talked in the parlor. Nearby were other nuns she knew, but before she could greet any of these, they began to move in procession down the corridor. Lighted candles were in their hands and they sang a joyful hymn as they walked.

"We go to the chapel now," whispered the Prioress, taking the child's hand in her own. "There you will receive the habit. Are you happy, little one?"

Imelda's blue eyes shone with a sudden and new-found joy. "Oh, yes, Mother. So happy!" What matter that a few minutes before the Devil had filled her heart with loneliness? That he had done his best to discourage her from leading a holy life? The temptation was over and done with now. She was about to give herself to God's service.

Presently the community was assembled in the chapel. The nuns knelt along the two walls, facing one another, while the Prioress took a chair near the iron grating which separated the chapel from the public church. Slowly the little newcomer approached and knelt at her feet.

"What do you ask?" inquired the superior gently.

Imelda's voice was confident. "God's mercy and yours."

At this, one of the nuns brought forward the white woolen tunic, scapular and linen veil of a Dominican novice, while a second began to cut the child's golden curls. All was very quiet. Imelda's young heart beat with excitement as she found herself being dressed in the religious habit. Soon she would be a real nun. Soon she would be *Sister Imelda!* What happiness! Nothing so wonderful had ever happened to her before!

But as the days passed, all was not sunshine in the new life. Sister Imelda soon learned that a novice must bear all manner of trials if she would persevere as a religious. She must learn humility and obedience and willingly act as the servant of others.

Imelda did her best to be humble and obedient, but sometimes she failed in other ways. One day she did not sweep the stairs carefully. On another she broke a dish. Again, she made a mistake in the chanting of the Office. All these faults had to be confessed in public, and the penance given by the Novice Mistress humbly performed. Certain of the older Sisters watched to see what Imelda would do when told to kneel before the community, either in the refectory or chapel, and recite the prayers imposed for such faults. Would she do so with a good grace? After all, the child came from a noble family. She was not used to humiliations.

"Have no fear about Sister Imelda," said the Prioress. "In all my days I have never seen a soul with a truer vocation."

The Novice Mistress agreed. "Our little sister would be a good one to look after the needs of the poor," she suggested one day. "Mother Prioress, will you give her permission for that?"

The Prioress hesitated. The convent of Saint Mary Magdalen was in the country. Many times rough wanderers appeared at the gate, their faces burned by the sun and wind, their clothes in rags. Perhaps the crude appearance of these poor souls would frighten such a little girl. Perhaps it would be better for one of the older nuns to attend to their needs. But when questioned on this point, Sister Imelda shook her head. She was not afraid of the poor, even of those who were ill of a dreadful disease. After all, a body that is sick or poorly clothed can never matter as much as the soul which it houses. Is the soul pleasing to God? That is the only question.

"And what if a great sinner should come to the gate some day?" asked the Prioress shrewdly. "The Devil would be in that soul, little one. Would you be afraid then?"

Imelda smiled in surprise. "Mother, how could I be afraid when God is in *me?*" she asked shyly. "I would pray for the sinner. I would ask God to drive away the Devil and leave the poor man in peace."

Such wisdom calmed the superior's fears and she agreed to let the young novice have charge of the poor who came to the monastery for food. The new duty delighted Imelda and she readily applied herself to the appointed task. A few days later, as she was reflecting upon her good fortune, a familiar voice caused her to look up in astonishment. The blind basket-maker had come to Val-di-Pietra! He was standing outside the gate!

"*Peter!* Is it really you?" she whispered.

The man chuckled. "Yes, little sister. I took a walk in the country today and a friend helped me up the hill. There was good reason to come, I think."

Imelda peered anxiously through the small barred window from which she gave food. Ordinarily she was required to have her face veiled when talking to outsiders, but she did not observe this custom when looking after the poor. The Prioress felt that some strangers might be a little timid at the sight of a veiled figure. Therefore Imelda had permission to see and be seen by all who came to her for help.

"Something's wrong at home," she said slowly. "That's why you've come. Oh, Peter! What is it? Tell me!"

The blind man caught the anxiety in his young friend's voice and quickly tried to reassure her. There was no bad news. Instead, he had come from Bologna to make a little gift.

"Twenty gold pieces, Sister," he said cheerfully. "See? They were given to me yesterday by a rich man."

Imelda sighed with relief, then gently shook her head at the sight of the glistening coins. "Peter, you know you can use this money yourself."

"And what about the Mother Prioress? Little sister, more than one beggar has been made happy by her generosity. Now give this money to her when you can. And don't forget to pray for me."

Unwillingly Imelda took the coins which Peter passed through the barred window. What could she say to this good friend? Time was growing short. Very soon the bell would call the community to choir. "Peter, I do pray for you," she said gently. "Every day. You know that. But I fear I can never pray for you or anyone as I really wish."

The blind man smiled. "As you wish? What do you mean, little sister?"

A sudden sadness clouded Imelda's blue eyes. "I mean with Our Lord in my heart. You see, the Sisters still think I am too young to understand about the Holy Eucharist. Oh, Peter! When will they let me make my First Communion? When will they let me pray for people as I really want to pray?"

The blind man was silent. He could not see his young friend, but the loneliness in her voice was heartbreaking. If anyone loved Our Lord, if anyone appreciated the mystery of the Holy Eucharist, surely it was this child of nine years.

UNWILLINGLY IMELDA TOOK THE COINS.

CHAPTER SIX

The Miracle

NFORTUNATELY these sentiments were not shared by the community. The nuns were kind to their little sister, but they respected tradition. As the months passed, Imelda realized that earthly power alone could not make her dream come true. No matter how hard she worked, how much she studied the Psalms, the Catechism, she could not receive Holy Communion before her fourteenth birthday.

In the spring of 1333, when she was eleven years old, the young Dominican wrote a little prayer. It was a simple one and intended for her own use. It ran as follows:

"You have said these words, dear Jesus: 'Permit the little ones to come to Me and forbid them not,' and You have made Yourself small so as to encourage us to approach You. Then why must my age keep me separated from You, especially when my soul loves You and desires You so much? Can Your loving heart remain deaf to my cries and prayers? When will I be able to say: 'I am coming to You'?"

Imelda said this prayer many times as she went about the tasks assigned to her by the Prioress. She also asked her two heavenly friends, Agnes and Tarcisius, to intercede for her with God. Sister Diana d'Andalo was not forgotten either, or Father Jordan of Saxony, the Dominican friar who had become Diana's friend and confessor after the death of Father Reginald of Orleans. No day passed that Imelda did not remind these faithful followers of Saint Dominic of her own great desire to receive Our Lord. But she did not speak of this to her sisters in religion, or to the poor who came to the monastery gate. After all, what could they do? It was God's Will that she suffer in silence—and wait.

Occasionally news of the outside world made its way into the quiet cloisters of Val-di-Pietra. For instance, there 'was trouble among the Visconti and the Malatesta, two noble families who were struggling to be rulers of Italy. Again, the Jews were being persecuted in several countries and many had fled to Spain and Portugal in order to save their lives. Lastly, two Italian writers, Petrarch and Boccaccio, were giving signs of literary genius. Although still young, many believed that some day these men would rival the great Dante himself.

However, the nuns knew less of these countrymen than they did of three foreigners living in the Rhineland—Henry Suso, John Tauler and John Ruysbroeck. They were teachers, preachers and writers of the Word of God. The first two were Dominican friars, and already tales had come to Valdi-Pietra of the great good they were accomplishing for souls. Some even believed them to be saints.

"These priests are true Dominicans," the nuns were told. "They pray, then they think and study about God and His Commandments. When the Holy Spirit has enlightened them, they go forth and preach to the people and write their books. It is really a wonderful vocation."

Imelda listened carefully to all that was said, happy in the thought that she also was a Dominican. Of course she did not preach sermons, teach in a University or write learned volumes. Yet all the same she was an important member of Saint Dominic's family. She and her sisters in religion prayed for the friars; they performed sacrifices in their humble cloister home, offering them to the Heavenly Father that He might receive them in the Name of His Son and bless those busy brothers in the pulpit and the classroom.

"Saint Dominic gathered together his nuns before he did anything else about founding a religious Order," thought the little girl. "He knew that preaching and teaching are necessary, but he also knew that prayer and sacrifice are the really important things when it comes to saving souls. Oh, I'm very glad I came here to Val-di-Pietra! It means I'm a missionary, too!"

Such knowledge served to comfort the child, particularly on the great feast of Easter when she, of all the community, was the only one who could not receive Our Lord in Holy Communion. And in the same way she was consoled when, some weeks later, the vigil of the feast of the Ascension was being observed. On this day, one of strict fast for members of the Dominican Order, Imelda's heart filled with new and unusual confidence. Something told her that God was pleased with so many years of patient waiting. Very soon He would grant her great desire.

"But how?" wondered the little girl. "Will You work a miracle, dear Lord? Will You let the Archbishop understand about things at last? And the Sisters?"

The questions were not answered, yet Imelda was happy as she assisted at Mass with the others. In a little while something really wonderful was going to happen. In some way, somehow, she was going to make her First Communion!

The minutes passed, and the priest read the Gospel, the Offertory prayers, the solemn words of Consecration. Imelda's eyes were radiant as she gazed upon the altar where the Sacred Hosts now rested in the golden chalice. She had only a side view of the altar, for it was in the public church attached to the monastery and obscured by the heavy iron grating which formed one end of the nuns' choir. However, neither iron bars nor distance could affect her faith and love. A few minutes ago God's power had transformed simple bread and wine into His own Body and Blood. Now whoever ate the Bread or drank the Wine was taking unto himself all Three Persons of the Most Blessed Trinity. It was truly a mystery beyond all human understanding as well as the greatest gift ever made to mankind.

"Even the angels can't receive Holy Communion,"

Imelda thought. "Or the saints in heaven. But any-
body who has the True Faith and who keeps the
Commandments can do so. Oh, I know the time has
come for me! I just know it!"

Presently a little bell rang three times. Imelda
turned hopefully toward the Prioress, confident that
the latter would smile and make some sign that she
was to join the others in approaching the Holy
Table. Alas! The superior did not even notice the
young novice. Her heavy linen veil was lowered, her
hands joined reverently. Slowly she rose to her feet
and led her sisters toward the far end of the chapel.
Then she gave the customary signal and immediately the community prostrated on the floor and
began to recite the *Confiteor* in muffled voices.

Imelda did not join them. She remained motion-
less in her place, gazing at the familiar scene with
tear-filled eyes. She had been wrong again! The little voice that had comforted her with the hope of
receiving Our Lord on this vigil of the Ascension
had been nothing but imagination. She was still
too small and ignorant to appreciate the Holy
Eucharist.

Soon the tears were falling freely. "Dear Lord,"
choked the little novice, "I . . . I love You! I love You!
That's all I know!"

When twenty minutes had passed and the nuns

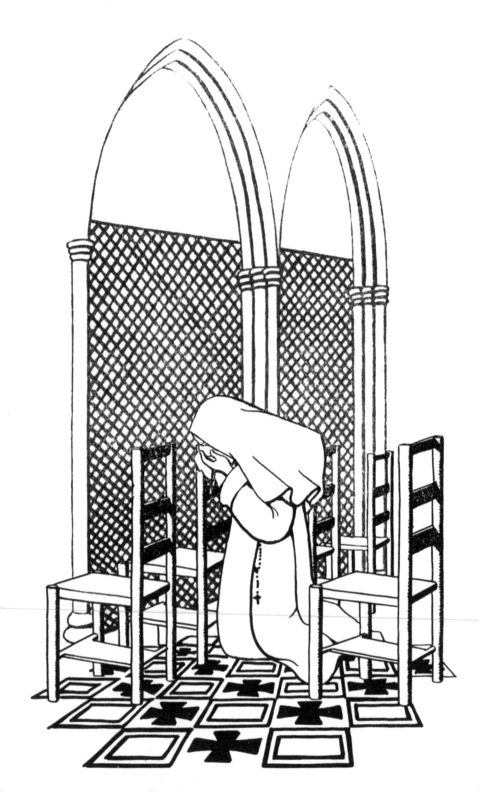

had completed their thanksgiving, Imelda still wept —her face hidden in her hands, her heart torn with disappointment and longing. Oh, why had she been so stupid? Why had she dared to hope that this day, this solemn vigil, would be the Great Day in her life?

There was sympathy in the eyes of a few older religious as they glanced briefly at their little sister. Poor child! Now that spring had come, she missed her mother. She was remembering the carefree days in her castle home when the gardens had been bright with rare flowers, when birds had fluttered down to feed from her hand and there was no promise of obedience that called for long hours of prayer and silence and work.

"The child was too young when she came to us," they thought. "It would have been better for her to have stayed a while in the world."

Imelda never guessed what her sisters were thinking. Indeed, the little novice was completely unaware of anything save the morning's great disappointment. She had not received Our Lord as she had hoped and prayed. What was there left to do now except to mourn?

So it was that she remained kneeling in the chapel long after the other nuns had departed. Once more she poured out her soul in words of fervent

---

IMELDA REMAINED BEHIND, WEEPING BITTERLY.

love, her eyes upon the altar where so recently the Holy Sacrifice had been offered.

"Dear Lord, I know You are truly present in this Tabernacle," she whispered. "I believe it with all my heart. But please don't stay hidden there. Come to me. I won't tell anyone of Your visit."

Suddenly the young novice became aware of a strange light playing about the distant altar. Against this light the heavy iron grating seemed to melt into thin air. She heard music, too—far away and indescribably sweet. As she gazed and listened, Imelda's heart almost burst with happiness. Just above the altar, suspended by an unseen power, was a Sacred Host! And it was moving! Moving toward her as a piece of steel moves toward a magnet!

"*Dear Lord!*" she gasped, her eyes upon the shining whiteness of the consecrated Bread. "*Dear Lord, are You coming to me?*"

As she knelt, not daring to move or breathe, the Sacred Host passed unhindered through the iron grating, then floated steadily down the nuns' chapel, nearer, nearer, until it came to rest just above Imelda's head. Carried out of herself, the little girl gazed in rapture. Our Lord had come!

Just then word was going through the monastery that young Sister Imelda was missing from her duties. She was not in her cell, not at the gate, not in

the garden. More than that. She had not come for
breakfast with the others.

"That child is never late for anything," thought
the Novice Mistress anxiously. "What can have happened to her?"

Since she remembered she had last seen the
young novice in the chapel, the good religious
decided to look for her missing charge here. But she
had not gone very far when she met the Prioress,
very breathless and excited.

"The flowers!" cried the Prioress. "Don't you smell
them, Mother? The whole house seems to be full of
roses and lilies!"

The Novice Mistress stopped, then sniffed the air.
It was true. There was a marvelous fragrance of
flowers everywhere about them.

"It must come from the garden," she said finally.
"It's spring again and we do have some lovely
flowers."

"But not enough to fill the whole house like this.
And so suddenly! Mother, I do believe the perfume is
coming from the chapel. Let's go and find out."

So the two religious hurried down the corridor,
marveling all the while that the delicate yet pene-
trating fragrance grew stronger as they neared the
chapel. But their curiosity was swept away as they
flung open the door. There, before their startled

eyes, was the missing Imelda. And over her head floated the Sacred Host!

"*My Lord and My God!*" gasped the Prioress, falling on her knees.

Attracted by the ever-increasing perfume of flowers and by the prolonged absence of the superior and her assistant, other members of the community presently arrived at the chapel. The same marvelous vision greeted them. Eleven-year-old Imelda was kneeling in ecstasy. She scarcely seemed to breathe. All that spoke of life was the radiance of her eyes as she gazed upon the Sacred Host just above her head.

As time passed and no change took place in the scene before them, the Novice Mistress felt that something should be done. She drew the Prioress away from the door.

"What are we going to do, Mother?" she whispered. "God must want our little sister to receive Him. But we . . . we can't give Him to her!"

The Prioress agreed. "Send word to the chaplain to come," she murmured. "Surely he will know what to do."

OVER HER HEAD FLOATED THE SACRED HOST.

CHAPTER SEVEN

LITTLE SAINT

HE chaplain was not long in making a decision. He had known of Sister Imelda's anxiety to receive Our Lord, and in his opinion the miracle could have but one meaning: the time had come for the child's great desire to be satisfied. Accordingly the good priest reverently approached Imelda, placed the Host on a golden paten, and gave the little novice her First Holy Communion.

It was the greatest event that had ever taken place within the monastery, and for more than an hour the nuns knelt in humble thanksgiving around their little sister. Finally the Prioress gave a signal.

HE GAVE THE LITTLE NOVICE HER FIRST HOLY COMMUNION.

All were to return to their duties.

"And Sister Imelda?" asked the Novice Mistress anxiously. "She . . . she is to come, too?"

The Prioress shook her head. "Let her stay, Mother. After all, she has waited so long for this happy day. She will have many things to say to Our Lord."

With a final glance at the little saint in their midst, the nuns took their departure. All were deeply moved. Imelda had always been a pretty child, but now she was beautiful beyond description. She seemed more like an angel than a little girl—a radiant angel reflecting all the splendors of heaven in her eyes.

"That's because God is within her," thought the Prioress. And as she knelt within the privacy of her own cell, the meaning of Holy Communion became clearer than ever before. It was the greatest privilege in the world—a proof, if one were needed, of God's immense love for all mankind.

"He gave us this great gift on the first Holy Thursday," she told herself. "He knew He would offer His life for the salvation of sinners, but at the Last Supper He decided that there was a way to save the world and yet remain with it. He turned ordinary bread and wine into His Body and Blood and told His disciples to eat and drink. Then He gave them the power to repeat this wonderful act. Ever since, we have had the Mass and the Holy Eucharist."

The Novice Mistress also was reflecting upon the meaning of the Blessed Sacrament. "We remember to feed our bodies each day," she thought. "If we don't, we finally grow sick and die. But the soul—ah, do we think to feed it as often as we can with the wonderful Food that is God Himself?"

As she meditated, an expression of sadness crossed the good nun's face. What a pity that the laws of the Church would not permit frequent Holy Communion! Surely if souls could approach the Holy Table once a week, or even every day, they would find it much easier to know and love God. They might even become saints in a very short time.

"The children should be allowed to come, too," she thought. "I know that now. Their souls need help as much as the souls of older people. Dear God, please hasten the day when boys and girls the world over can come to You while they are still very small!"

From time to time the nuns returned to the chapel to gaze on their little sister, who was still absorbed in prayer. It seemed as if she had not moved since the moment of the great miracle. She was still kneeling in the very spot where she had assisted at Mass.

"She looks like a little white statue," whispered

one religious in an awed voice. "I . . . I have never seen anything like it!"

"Yes, but she shouldn't be kneeling so long," put in another anxiously. "Perhaps we should go and tell her. . . ."

"No, don't bother her," a third hastened to add. "It wouldn't be right after what happened this morning."

So the nuns contented themselves with occasional visits to the chapel, glancing each time at Imelda and marveling at the radiant peace upon her uplifted face. It was almost as though she still saw the Sacred Host floating above her, waiting to be received into its human Tabernacle. And as the community watched their little sister, they recalled the words she had spoken only recently.

"How can anyone receive Our Lord and not die of happiness?"

There were other things Imelda had said, too. In her own childlike way, she had told her sisters that the Blessed Sacrament was like a wonderful medicine. It made souls strong against temptation. It brought hope to the fearful and comfort to the weary. It also brought an opportunity to know God better.

"We can only love what we know," the child had said, "and so we ought to do all we can to know God.

Then it will be very easy to love Him and to do His Will."

The Prioress was thinking of these words as she came once more to the chapel. Imelda was still kneeling in prayer, but now there seemed to be a certain weariness about the little figure.

"She's tired from kneeling so long," she told herself. "I'd better go and say it's time to leave."

As the superior approached the scene of the recent miracle, she stretched out a gentle hand. "Sister Imelda," she whispered softly. "Come along now, child. You've prayed long enough."

But there was no answer, and suddenly the Prioress felt a stab of pain. The face of the little novice was so pale! It almost seemed. . . .

"*Sister Imelda!*" she cried anxiously. "Sister Imelda, look at me!"

Again there was no answer. By now the Prioress was thoroughly alarmed, and took the young novice by the shoulders. At once the little form slipped back into her arms. The child was dead!

"Holy Mother of God!" cried the Prioress, as she caught the limp little body, "I must be dreaming!"

But it was no dream. Imelda had died a few minutes after making her First Communion.

Before long the breathtaking story was spreading throughout the countryside. Men and women flocked to the monastery from cottages and farms, finally even from the great city of Bologna itself. All clamored for the truth. What had caused the death of Sister Imelda? Had she been ill? Had she suffered some sudden accident?

"The child died of joy," announced the Prioress, her heart aglow with a strange excitement that left no room for sorrow. "She finished the work God gave her to do and now she has left us. Oh, my friends, some day the whole world will know this wonderful story!"

As best she could, the superior then described the miracle that had occurred that morning. Our Lord had come to Sister Imelda in an extraordinary way. He had given proof that He did not wish little children to be kept from Him. He wished to enter their hearts and help them to be strong and good.

"But the laws of the Church. . . ." ventured a certain priest. "They do not permit Holy Communion for boys and girls. You know that, Mother Prioress."

"Yes, Father, but some day there will be a change. Little Imelda gave her life for this favor, and God will not refuse her anything. I know it!"

There was such conviction in the good nun's voice that the priest was impressed in spite of himself. Perhaps the Prioress was right. Maybe a day would come when children might approach the Holy Eucharist at an early age. Of course it would take time. No doubt centuries would have to pass before such a wonderful thing was possible. In the end, however, the Church would decide to let boys and girls receive Our Lord while they were still quite small.

"The older people mustn't be forgotten either," thought the priest. "How wonderful if they could have permission to receive Holy Communion every day! Little Imelda, will you ask God to grant this great favor, too?"

Even as he uttered this prayer, there was a slight commotion outside and a low murmur spread through the crowd gathered in the monastery grounds. The Captain General of Bologna had just arrived with his wife.

"*The child's parents!*" exclaimed the priest. "Mother Prioress, what are you going to say to them?"

The eyes of the superior were anxious as she gazed through the iron grating of the parlor. "I can only tell them the truth," she whispered. "Father, will you pray that they receive it well?"

There was no need for anxiety, however. The first wonder Imelda had worked upon reaching Paradise was to secure for her parents the gift of accepting God's Will with eagerness and trust. Of course the father and mother were grieved at losing their only child but they did not question or complain. God had some wonderful plan in store for their little one.

Some day they would understand just what it was.

"Perhaps we could see her now?" asked Donna Castora, dry-eyed and calm.

The Prioress nodded quickly. "Of course, my lady. Her body is in the nuns' chapel. You can see it if you go into the public church and kneel by the grating."

The nun had bowed and was about to make her departure when the Captain General held out a restraining hand. "The child didn't . . . didn't suffer, Mother Prioress? She died without any pain?"

The superior smiled. "It was so peaceful a death that no one knew about it for a long time. Sister Imelda was just kneeling in her usual place . . . smiling and joyous about her First Communion . . . oh, there are no words to describe how your little girl went to God! Just go and look at her now and you may understand what I mean."

So the Captain General and his wife took leave of the Prioress and made their way into the crowded public church. At once an excited whisper arose from all sides.

"The little saint's parents have come! Make way, everybody!"

The onlookers withdrew, and presently Donna Castora was walking up the center aisle on her husband's arm. She scarcely noticed the eager glances, the excited murmurs. Her mind was filled with but one thought. Her little girl was dead, yet she herself was experiencing the most wonderful happiness!

"It was the same when we brought her here two years ago," she marveled silently. "At first I felt my heart would break when Imelda wanted to leave us and give herself to God. Then I learned the truth: no one is ever the loser when he makes the Heavenly Father a present. The smallest gift comes back a hundredfold. I gave my child to God, and now He has given her back to me—*a saint!*"

For over an hour the parents knelt beside the iron grating, gazing at the still body of their little daughter. How peaceful she seemed, how beautiful, in the white woolen habit of the Dominican Order! Someone had placed a wreath of snowy roses on her head, but the fragrance filling the air was not from these. It was too sweet a perfume to come from anywhere save heaven.

"This child belongs to the whole world," thought Donna Castora joyfully. "God means her to be a little missionary and bring many souls to Him. Oh, Imelda!"

Suddenly the reverent hush in the church was broken. A grey-haired man had forced his way through the crowd and now insisted on entering the sanctuary to pray beside the grating. The fact that Imelda's parents were already here did not deter him. When a dozen men rushed forward to hold him back, he turned on them almost fiercely.

"Let me be!" he cried. "Don't you know that I have a . . . *a duty* to perform?"

Hearing the commotion behind her, Donna Castora turned. Immediately the color drained from her face and she clutched her husband's arm. "Egano!" she whispered unbelievingly. "Egano, look!"

As she spoke, the grey-haired man sprang through the crowd and entered the sanctuary. The Captain General rose unsteadily to his feet. "Why, it's the basket-maker!" he cried. "And he's walking without his cane!"

With scarcely a glance at the richly-dressed man and woman, the newcomer flung himself on his knees before the grating. For several minutes he knelt in prayer, his eyes upon the small white-clad figure in the nuns' chapel. Then, as Donna Castora and her husband stared in blank amazement, he turned toward them.

"*I can see!*" he whispered softly.

New York City
Feast of the Solemnity of Saint Joseph
April 26, 1944

PRAYER

O LORD Jesus Christ, Who didst receive into Heaven the blessed virgin Imelda, wounded with the burning love of Thy charity and wonderfully sustained by an immaculate Host, grant us through her intercession to approach the Holy Table with a like fervor of charity, that we may long to be dissolved and to be with Thee, Who livest and reignest, world without end. Amen.

HISTORICAL NOTE

Blessed Imelda lived from 1322-1333, Pope Leo XII formally approved the veneration of Imelda as a Blessed on December 20, 1826, and granted the Dominican Order and the diocese of Bologna the privilege of a Mass and Office in her honor, Her feasts used to be celebrated on May 12 and September 16, although they are no longer officially observed. Her relics lie in the little church of St. Sigismund in Bologna,

In 1891 the Bishop of Carcassonne established a confraternity in honor of Blessed Imelda, known as "The Confraternity or Sodality of a Good First Communion and of Perseverance." Pope Leo XII raised the Confraternity to the status of an Archconfraternity, but this organization is now no longer active.

Pope St. Pius X (1903-1914) declared Blessed Imelda the Patroness of First Communicants, (St. Tarsicius is the Patron of First Communicants.)